Just Ducky

Combine the traditional Duck & Ducklings blocks with appliquéd ducks to make this sunny quilt for Baby.

Project Specifications

Quilt Size: 39" x 51"
Block Size: 6" x 6"
Number of Blocks: 27

Fabrics & Batting

- 5/8 yard gold solid
- 1 yard each green and yellow prints
- 1 1/2 yards yellow plaid
- 1 yard white-on-white print
- Backing 43" x 55"
- Quilter's fleece 43" x 55"

Tools & Supplies

- All-purpose thread to match fabrics
- Green, gold and yellow machine-embroidery thread
- Cream machine-quilting thread
- 1/2 yard fusible transfer web
- 5/8 yard fabric stabilizer
- Basting spray
- Basic sewing tools and supplies, rotary cutter, mat and ruler

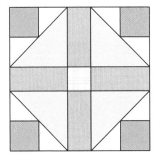

Duck & Ducklings
6" x 6" Block

Instructions

1. Cut two strips each 2 1/2" x 39 1/2" and 2 1/2" x 47 1/2" and one strip 1 1/2" x 45" along length of yellow plaid. Set aside.

2. Cut two strips white-on-white print 6 1/2" by fabric width; subcut into eight 6 1/2" squares.

3. Trace duck pieces onto the paper side of the fusible transfer web referring to the patterns for the number to be traced. Cut out leaving a margin around each shape.

4. Fuse shapes onto back of fabrics referring to patterns for color and following manufacturer's instructions; cut out on traced lines. Remove paper backing.

5. Arrange shapes for one duck on each white-on-white print square referring to Placement Diagram for positioning of pieces; fuse in place.

6. Cut a piece of fabric stabilizer to fit behind duck shape.

7. Machine-appliqué shapes in place using machine-embroidery thread to match fabrics in the top of the machine and all-purpose thread in the bobbin. Remove fabric stabilizer.

8. Cut seven strips 2 1/8" by fabric width white-on-white print; subcut each strip into 2 1/8" square segments. Cut each square on one diagonal to make A triangles. You will need 256 A triangles.

9. Cut six strips 1 3/4" by fabric width gold solid; subcut each strip into 1 3/4" square segments for B. You will need 128 B squares.

10. Cut 6 strips 3 3/8" by fabric width yellow print; subcut each strip into 3 3/8" square segments. Cut each square on one diagonal to make C triangles. You will need 128 C triangles.

11. Cut five strips green print 3" by fabric width; subcut three strips into 1 1/2" segments to make D rectangles. You will need 62 D rectangles. Set aside remaining strips.

12. Sew the 1 1/2"-wide yellow plaid strip cut in step 1 between the remaining green print strips to make a strip set as shown in Figure 1.

13. Cut the strip set into 1 1/2" segments for E, again referring to Figure 1. You will need 27 E segments.

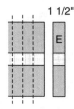

Figure 1
Sew the yellow plaid strip between the green print strips; cut into 1 1/2" segments for E.

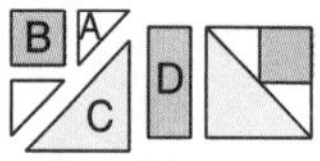

Figure 2
Sew A to adjacent sides of B; add C. Sew to opposite sides of D.

14. To piece one Duck & Ducklings block, sew A to adjacent sides of B as shown in Figure 2; add C. Repeat for four A-B-C units.

15. Sew an A-B-C unit to opposite sides of D as shown in Figure 2; repeat.

16. Sew E between the two pieced units to complete one block as shown in Figure 3; repeat to make 27 blocks.

Figure 3
Sew E between the 2 pieced units to complete 1 block

17. To piece one half-block unit, repeat steps 14 and 15. Repeat to make eight half-block units.

18. Join three blocks to make a row; repeat for five rows.

19. Join the rows to complete the center section.

20. Cut two strips each yellow plaid 3" x 18 1/2" and 3" x 30 1/2". Sew the longer strips to

opposite sides of the center section; press seams toward strips.

21. Complete four A-B-C units referring to step 14. Sew an A-B-C unit to opposite ends of the shorter yellow plaid strips as shown in Figure 4; sew a strip to the remaining sides of the center section.

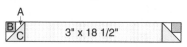

Figure 4
Sew an A-B-C unit to opposite ends of the yellow plaid strips.

22. Join three duck squares with two Duck & Ducklings blocks and two half-block units to make a strip as shown in Figure 5; repeat.

Figure 5
Join 3 duck squares with 2 blocks and 2 half-block units to make a strip.

23. Sew a block strip to opposite long sides of the bordered center section referring to the Placement Diagram for positioning of strips.

24. Join one duck square with four Duck & Ducklings blocks and two half-block units to make a strip as shown in Figure 6; repeat.

25. Sew a block strip to the remaining sides of the bordered center section to complete the top referring to the Placement Diagram for positioning of strips.

Figure 6
Join 1 duck square with 4 blocks and 2 half-block units to make a strip.

26. Sew the 2 1/2" x 47 1/2" yellow plaid strips cut in step 1 to opposite sides of the pieced center; sew the 2 1/2" x 39 1/2" strips to the top and bottom. Press seams toward strips to complete the top.

27. Spray one side of quilter's fleece with basting spray; place wrong side of prepared backing on sprayed side. Repeat on opposite side of quilter's fleece with completed top.

28. Hand- or machine-quilt as desired. Note: *The sample shown was machine-quilted in an allover meandering*

pattern using cream machine-quilting thread in the top of the machine and all-purpose thread in the bobbin.

29. When quilting is complete, remove pins or basting; trim edges even with top. Cut five strips 2 1/4" by fabric width green print. Join strips on short ends to make a long strip. Fold the strip in half with wrong sides together; press to make binding strip. Bind edges of quilt to finish. ❖

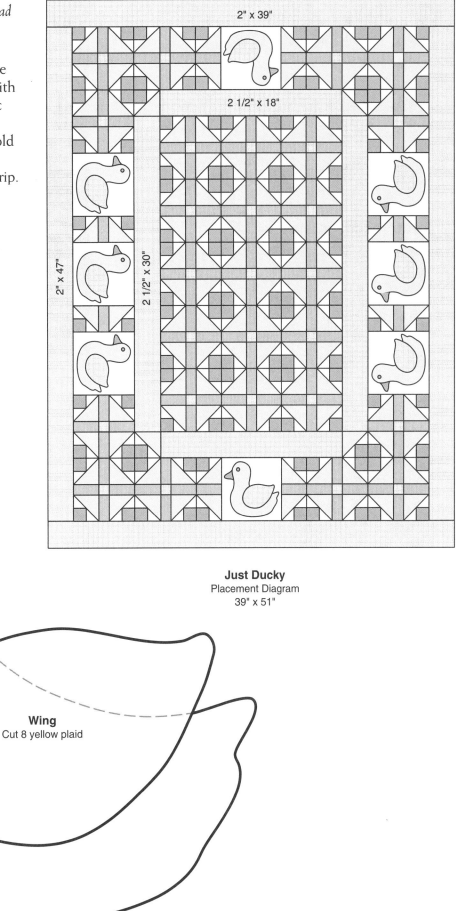

Just Ducky
Placement Diagram
39" x 51"

Eye
Cut 8 green print

Bill
Cut 8 gold solid

Duck
Cut 8 yellow print

Wing
Cut 8 yellow plaid

Twinkling Stars

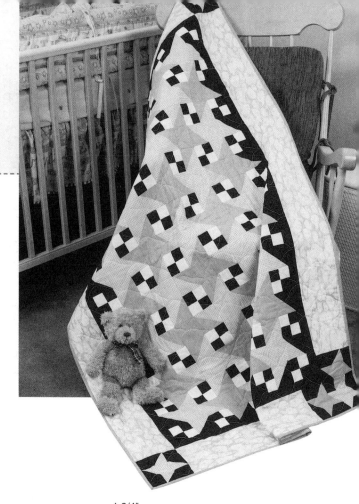

Sashing creates the light blue stars scattered across this celestial quilt.

Project Specifications

Quilt Size: 38 1/2" x 58 1/2"
Block Size: 4 1/2" x 4 1/2" and 7 1/2" x 7 1/2"
Number of Blocks: 4 and 15

Fabrics & Batting

- 3/8 yard white-on-white print
- 3/4 yard cloud print
- 1 yard each yellow check and light blue and navy prints
- Backing 43" x 63"
- Quilter's fleece 43" x 63"

Tools & Supplies

- All-purpose thread to match fabrics
- Basic sewing tools and supplies, rotary cutter, mat and ruler

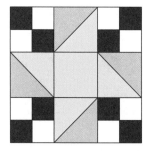

Twinkling Star
7 1/2" x 7 1/2" Block

Simple Star
4 1/2" x 4 1/2" Block

Instructions

1. Cut five strips each navy and white-on-white prints 1 3/4" by fabric width.

2. Sew a navy strip to a white strip along length to make a strip set; repeat for five strip sets.

3. Cut each strip set into 1 3/4" segments as shown in Figure 1; you will need 120 segments.

4. Join two pieced segments to make a Four-Patch unit as shown in Figure 2; repeat to make 60 Four-Patch units.

1 3/4"

Figure 1
Cut each strip set
into 1 3/4" segments.

Figure 2
Join 2 segments to
make a Four-Patch unit.

5. Cut four strips each yellow check and light blue print and two strips navy print 3 3/8" by fabric width; subcut each strip into 3 3/8" square segments for A. You will need 14 navy, 44 light blue and 46 yellow A squares.

6. Draw a diagonal line on the wrong side of all yellow A squares and 12 light blue A squares.

7. Place a yellow A square right sides together with a navy A square; stitch 1/4" from each side of the marked line as shown in Figure 3. Cut apart on the marked line; press open to make two yellow/navy A units as shown in Figure 4.

1/4"

Figure 3
Stitch 1/4" from each
side of the marked line.

Figure 4
Cut apart on the marked line;
press open to make A units.

8. Repeat step 7 to make 16 yellow/navy, 12 light blue/navy and 76 yellow/light blue A units as shown in Figure 5.

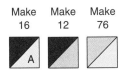

Make 16 Make 12 Make 76

Figure 5
Make A units in color combinations shown.

9. Cut two strips each yellow check and light blue print 3" by fabric width; subcut each strip into 3" square segments for B. You will need 22 light blue and 23 yellow B squares.

10. To piece one Twinkling Star block, sew a yellow/light blue A unit between two Four-Patch units to make a row as shown in Figure 6; repeat.

Figure 6
Sew a yellow/light blue A unit between 2 Four-Patch units to make a row.

Figure 7
Sew a yellow B between 2 yellow/light blue A units to make a row.

11. Sew a yellow B square between two yellow/light blue A units to make a row as shown in Figure 7.

12. Join the rows to complete one block as shown in Figure 8; repeat to make 15 blocks in color combinations as shown in Figure 9.

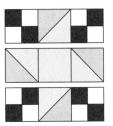

Figure 8
Join the rows to complete 1 Twinkling Star block.

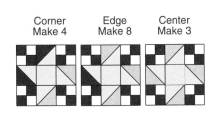

Corner Make 4   Edge Make 8   Center Make 3

Figure 9
Make 15 blocks in the color combinations shown.

Figure 10
Sew a light blue B between 2 yellow/light blue A units to make a sashing strip.

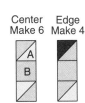

Center Make 6   Edge Make 4

Figure 11
Make 10 sashing strips in the color combinations shown.

13. Sew a light blue B square between two yellow/light blue A units to make a sashing strip as shown in Figure 10; repeat to make 10 sashing strips in color combinations as shown in Figure 11.

14. Join two corner blocks, one edge block and two edge sashing units to make block row A as shown in Figure 12; repeat for two A block rows.

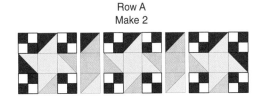

Row A
Make 2

Figure 12
Join blocks and sashing strips to make block row A.

15. Join two edge blocks, one center block and two center sashing units to make block row B as shown in Figure 13; repeat for three B block rows.

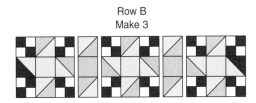

Row B
Make 3

Figure 13
Join blocks and sashing strips to make block row B.

16. Join two light blue/navy A units, four yellow/light blue A units, two yellow B squares and three light blue B squares to make a sashing row as shown in Figure 14; repeat for four sashing rows.

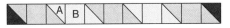

Figure 14
Join A units and B squares to make a sashing row.

17. Join A and B block rows with the sashing rows to complete the pieced center, beginning and ending with an A block row and referring to Figure 15 for positioning of rows.

18. Cut (and piece) two strips each 1 1/2" x 30" and 1 1/2" x 48" navy print; sew the longer strips to opposite long sides of the pieced center and shorter strips to the top and bottom. Press seams toward strips.

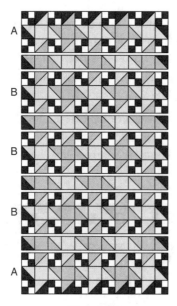

Figure 15
Join A and B block rows with
sashing rows as shown.

19. Cut one strip each 2" by fabric width and 2 3/8" by fabric width navy print; subcut into twenty-four 2" square segments for B and twelve 2 3/8" square segments for A.

20. Cut eight squares each light blue print and yellow check 2 3/8" x 2 3/8" for A and four squares each color 2" x 2" for B.

21. Draw a diagonal line on the wrong side of all yellow A squares and six light blue A squares.

22. Make 12 yellow/navy, 12 light blue/navy and 4 yellow/light blue A units referring to step 7.

23. To piece one Simple Star block, join two navy B squares with one yellow/navy A unit to make a row as shown in Figure 16; repeat.

24. Join one yellow B square with two yellow/navy A units to make a row, again referring to Figure 16.

Figure 16
Join A units and B
squares in rows; join
rows to complete 1
Simple Star block.

Make 2   Make 2

Figure 17
Make blocks in color
combinations shown.

25. Join the rows to complete one block; repeat to make four blocks in color combinations as shown in Figure 17.

26. Join two navy B squares with one light blue/navy A unit as shown in Figure 18. Join one light blue B square with two light blue/navy A units referring to Figure 18. Join the two pieced strips to make a border unit, again referring to Figure 18; repeat for four border units.

Figure 18
Join A units and
B squares to
make border
units as shown.

5" x 47"

Figure 19
Sew a border unit to 1 end of a longer strip.

27. Cut (and piece) two strips each 5" x 27" and 5" x 47" cloud print.

28. Sew a border unit to one end of each longer cloud print strip as shown in Figure 19; sew a strip to opposite long sides of the pieced center.

29. Sew a border unit to one end and a Simple Star block to the opposite end of each shorter cloud print strip as shown in Figure 20; sew a strip to the top and bottom of the pieced center to complete the top referring to the Placement Diagram for positioning of strips.

5" x 27"

Figure 20
Sew a border unit and Simple
Star block to opposite ends of
a shorter strip.

30. Sandwich quilter's fleece between the top and the prepared backing piece; pin or baste to hold.

31. Hand- or machine-quilt as desired. Note: *The sample shown was professionally machine-quilted in an allover meandering pattern.*

32. When quilting is complete, remove pins or basting and trim edges even. Cut five strips 2 1/4" by fabric width light blue print. Join strips on short ends to make a long strip. Fold strip in half along length with wrong sides together; press to make binding strip. Bind edges of quilt to finish.❖

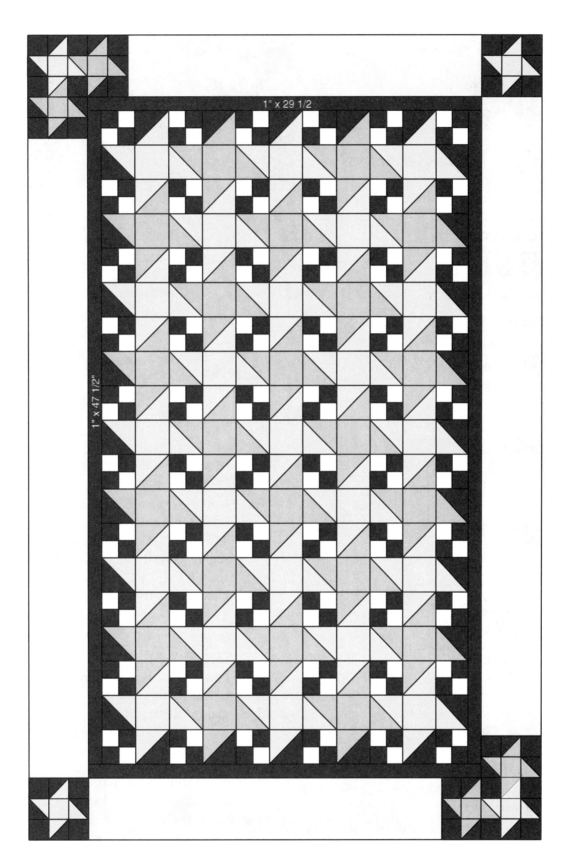

Twinkling Stars
Placement Diagram
38 1/2" x 58 1/2"

Pinwheel Basics

Introduce Baby to the basics with this bright-colored quilt.

Project Specifications
Quilt Size: 34 1/2" x 55"
Block Size: 3" x 5", 5" x 5" and 6" x 6"
Number of Blocks: 9, 9 and 12

Fabrics & Batting
- 1/4 yard yellow print
- 1/2 yard each 8 bright prints
- 2 1/2 yards white print
- Backing 39" x 59"
- Quilter's fleece 39" x 59"

Tools & Supplies
- All-purpose thread to match fabrics
- White, red and yellow machine-quilting thread
- Basic sewing tools and supplies, rotary cutter, mat and ruler

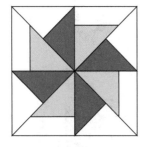

Pinwheel
6" x 6" Block

Instructions
1. Prepare templates for pattern pieces given; cut as directed on each piece.
2. Cut two strips 4 1/4" by fabric width white print; subcut into 4 1/4" square segments. Cut each square on both diagonals to make B triangles. You will need 48 white B triangles.
3. Cut two strips 3" by fabric width yellow print; subcut into 3" square segments. Cut each square on one diagonal to make C triangles. You will need 48 C triangles.
4. Cut two strips 7" by fabric width white print; subcut into three 1 1/2" x 7" segments for G, two 1 3/4" x 6 1/2" segments for H, two 1" x 6 1/2" segments for J, two 1 3/4" x 7" segments for K, six 4 1/2" x 5 1/2" segments for L and six 4 1/2" x 7" segments for M.
5. To piece one Pinwheel block, cut one square bright print 4 1/4" x 4 1/4". Cut the square on both diagonals to make bright B triangles.
6. Sew a white B to a bright B as shown in Figure 1; repeat for four B units.
7. Sew A to C as shown in Figure 2; repeat for four A-C units.
8. Sew an A-C unit to a B unit as shown in Figure 3; repeat for four A-B-C units.

Figure 1
Sew a white B to a bright B.

Figure 2
Sew A to C.

Figure 3
Sew an A-C unit to a B unit.

9. Join the A-B-C units to complete one block as shown in Figure 4.

Figure 4
Join the A-B-C units
to complete 1 block.

10. Repeat steps 5–8 to make 12 Pinwheel blocks, one each of four bright prints and two each of four bright prints.

11. Cut two strips 6 1/2" by fabric width white print; subcut into 6 1/2" squares.

12. Join two Pinwheel blocks with one white print square to make a row as shown in Figure 5; repeat for three rows.

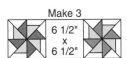

Figure 5
Join 2 Pinwheel blocks with
1 square to make a row.

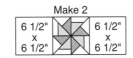

Figure 6
Join 2 squares with 1
Pinwheel block to make a row.

13. Join two white print squares with one Pinwheel block to make a row as shown in Figure 6; repeat for two rows. Set aside remaining Pinwheel blocks.

14. Join rows to complete the center rectangle as shown in Figure 7.

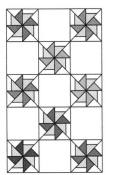

Figure 7
Join rows to complete
the center rectangle.

Figure 8
Fold a square diagonally;
fold a second time to
make a prairie point.

15. Cut one strip each bright print 3 1/2" by fabric width; subcut strips into 3 1/2" square segments. You will need 92 bright print squares.

16. Fold each square diagonally with wrong sides together as shown in Figure 8; press. Fold a second time to make prairie points, again referring to Figure 8; press.

17. Arrange six prairie points along each short edge of the center rectangle and 10 along each long edge as shown in Figure 9; pin in place. Machine-baste along edge using a 1/8" seam allowance.

Figure 9
Arrange prairie points along
edges of center rectangle.

18. Cut two strips each 2 1/2" x 22 1/2" and 2 1/2" x 30 1/2" white print. Sew the longer strips to opposite long sides of the center rectangle and the shorter strips to the top and bottom to complete the center unit; press seams toward center rectangle, folding prairie points out to lay against white print strips.

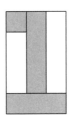

1
3" x 5" Block

2
3" x 5" Block

3
3" x 5" Block

19. Make paper patterns for A, B, C, 1, 2 and 3 blocks in numbers as directed on patterns. Paper-piece three of each block using only one bright print in a block and referring to Paper-Piecing Hints. Do not remove paper patterns.

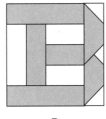
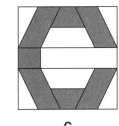

A
5" x 5" Block

B
5" x 5" Block

C
5" x 5" Block

20. To border one letter block, place D right sides together on one block edge; stitch seam stopping 1" from end of block as shown in Figure 10. Place a second D along an adjacent block edge; stitch seam as shown in Figure 11. Continue to add D pieces around block, stitching remainder of partial first seam to complete the block border as shown in Figure 12.

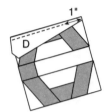

Figure 10
Stitch seam stopping 1" from end of block.

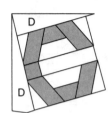

Figure 11
Stitch seam of second D as shown.

Figure 12
Stitch remainder of partial seam to complete block border.

21. Repeat step 20 with D and DR pieces to make bordered blocks as shown in Figure 13. Remove paper patterns.

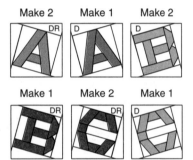

Figure 13
Complete bordered letter blocks as shown.

22. To border one number block, sew E to opposite long sides of the block as shown in Figure 14. Sew F to the top and bottom to complete the block border, again referring to Figure 14.

Figure 14
Sew E to opposite sides of a number block; add F to the top and bottom.

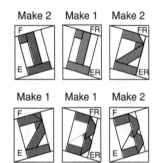

Figure 15
Complete bordered number blocks as shown.

23. Repeat step 22 with E and F and ER and FR pieces to make bordered blocks as shown in Figure 15. Remove paper patterns.

24. Sew G to one side of one each 1, 2 and 3 bordered blocks as shown in Figure 16. Join with two Pinwheel blocks and two H segments to make a strip as shown in Figure 17.

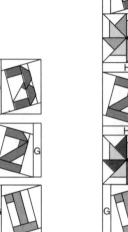
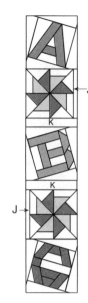

Figure 16
Sew G to 1 side of 3 number blocks.

Figure 17
Join blocks with 2 Pinwheel blocks and 2 H segments.

Figure 18
Join 1 each letter block with 2 Pinwheel blocks and 2 K segments.

25. Sew J to one side of two Pinwheel blocks as shown in Figure 18. Join one each A, B and C bordered blocks with the two Pinwheel blocks and two K segments to make a strip, again referring to Figure 18.

26. Sew the number and letter strips to opposite sides of the center unit referring to the Placement Diagram for positioning of strips.

27. Sew an M strip to one end of each bordered letter block and an L strip to one end of each bordered number block as shown in Figure 19 and referring to the Placement Diagram for positioning on each block.

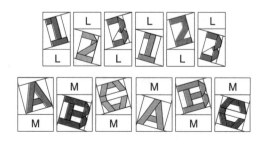

Figure 19
Sew an M strip to 1 end of each letter block and an L strip to 1 end of each number block.

28. Join number and letter units to make two strips as shown in Figure 20. Sew a strip to the top and bottom of the center unit to complete the pieced top referring to the Placement Diagram for positioning of strips.

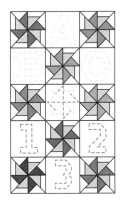

Figure 21
Quilt white print squares as shown.

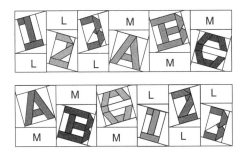

Figure 20
Join number and letter units to make 2 strips.

29. Arrange 12 prairie points along each short edge of the completed top and 18 along each long edge as for center rectangle; pin in place and machine-baste.

30. Place prepared backing piece on quilter's fleece; place completed top right sides together with backing piece with basted prairie points on inside of layers. Pin to hold.

31. Stitch all around edge leaving a 6" opening for turning; remove pins. Turn right side out through opening pulling prairie point ends out away from quilt. Hand-stitch opening closed.

32. Hand- or machine-quilt as desired to finish. **Note:** *The sample shown was machine-quilted using the paper-piecing number and letter patterns as guides for quilting in the white print squares and using red machine-quilting thread in the top of the machine and white all-purpose thread in the bobbin for the numbers and yellow machine-quilting thread for the letters as shown in Figure 21. A pinwheel shape was machine-quilted in the last white print square using both red and yellow machine-quilting thread, again referring to Figure 21. The remainder was machine-quilted in the ditch of seams around letters, numbers and pinwheels using white machine-quilting thread.* ❖

Pinwheel Basics
Placement Diagram
34 1/2" x 55"

Paper-Piecing Hints

- Shorten stitch length to 15–18 stitches per inch.
- Use thread to match bright print in each block.
- Place specified fabric to cover section 1 on paper pattern with wrong side of fabric against unmarked side of paper and allowing fabric edges to extend at least 1/4" into adjacent sections.
- Place specified fabric for section 2 right sides together with fabric 1 on the 1-2 edge; pin along the 1-2 line. Fold fabric 2 to cover section 2, again allowing fabric to extend at least 1/4" into adjacent sections. Adjust fabric if necessary. Unfold fabric 2 to lie flat on fabric 1.
- Flip paper pattern; stitch on the 1–2 line beginning and ending 2 or 3 stitches into adjacent sections and stitching to outside heavy line on edge sections.
- Trim 1–2 seam allowance. Fold fabric 2 to cover section 2; lightly press with a warm dry iron.
- Continue to add fabrics to sections in numerical order to cover paper pattern.
- Trim paper and fabric edges even on outside heavy line.
- Join block sections to complete the block if necessary.
- Leave paper pattern intact until joined with other pieces.

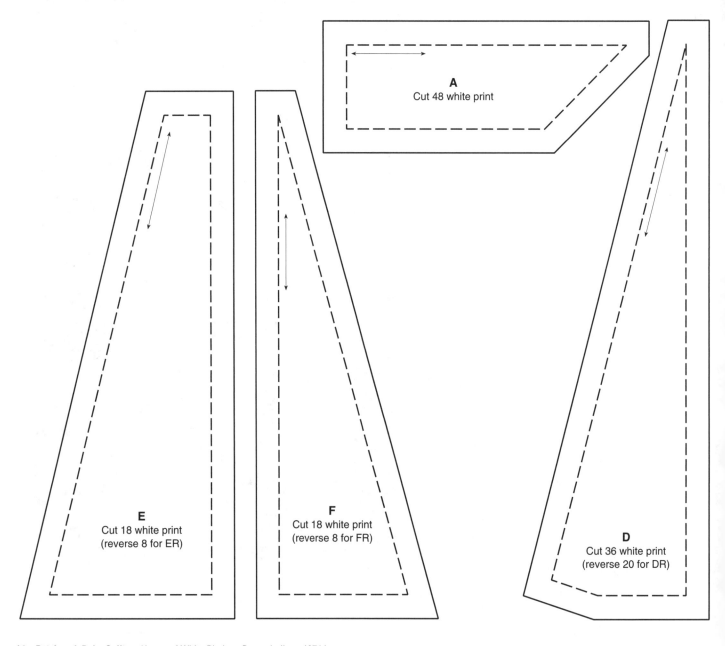

A
Cut 48 white print

E
Cut 18 white print
(reverse 8 for ER)

F
Cut 18 white print
(reverse 8 for FR)

D
Cut 36 white print
(reverse 20 for DR)

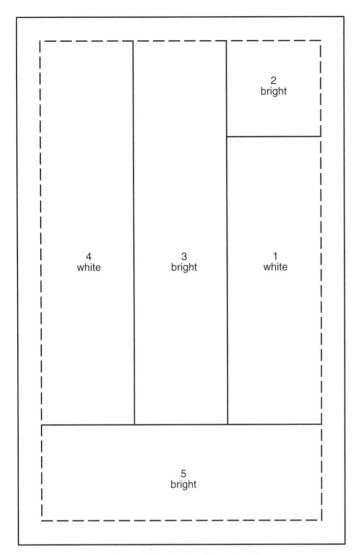

Paper-Piecing Pattern for 1
Make 3

Paper-Piecing Pattern for 3A
Make 3

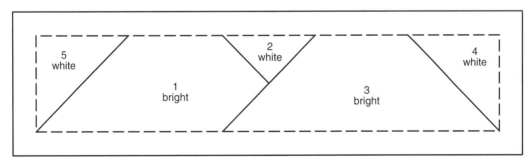

Paper-Piecing Pattern for B2 & 3B
Make 6

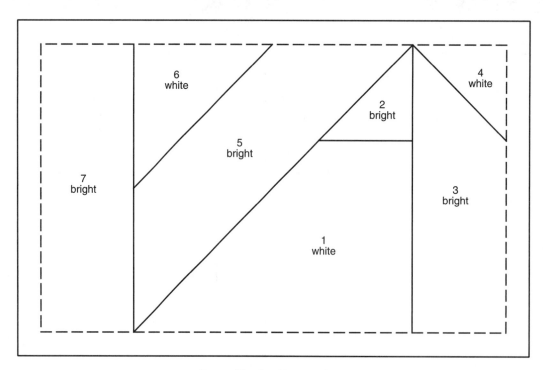

Paper-Piecing Pattern for 2
Make 3

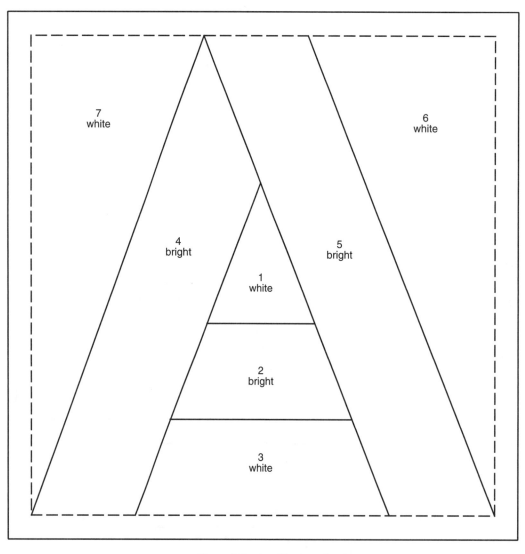

Paper-Piecing Pattern for A
Make 3

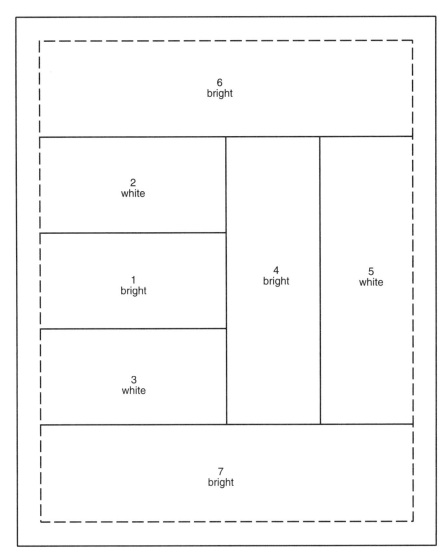

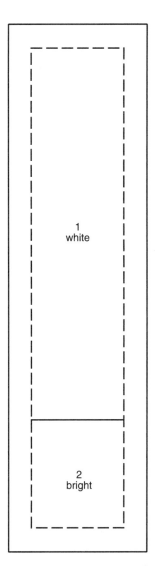

Paper-Piecing Pattern for B1
Make 3

Paper-Piecing Pattern for C2
Make 3

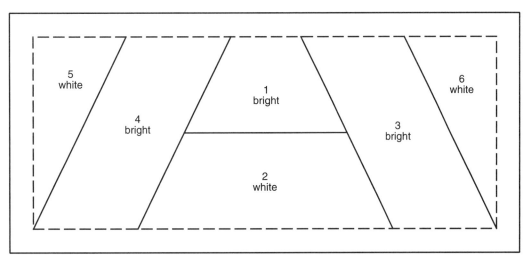

Paper-Piecing Pattern for C1
Make 6

Little Ballerina

Pastel-colored chintz prints make a soft frame for this little teddy bear ballerina.

Project Specifications
Quilt Size: 35" x 50"

Fabrics & Batting
- Scrap each black and pink solids and tan print
- 1/4 yard each blue, yellow, green and lilac dot
- 1/3 yard brown print
- 3/8 yard pink dot
- 1/2 yard muslin
- 1 3/4 yards each white print and pink floral
- Backing 38" x 53"
- Quilter's fleece 38" x 53"

Tools & Supplies
- All-purpose thread to match fabrics
- Brown, light pink, dark pink, black and white machine-embroidery thread
- Pastel-variegated rayon thread
- Pink and white machine-quilting thread
- 2 1/2 yards fusible transfer web
- 2 1/2 yards fabric stabilizer
- 5 yards white 2 1/2"-wide eyelet ruffle
- Basic sewing tools and supplies, press cloth, chalk pencil, rotary cutter, mat and ruler

Instructions

1. Cut a 35 1/2" x 50 1/2" rectangle pink floral. Fold in half along length; fold in half to form quarters. Trim corner into round shape to make background piece as shown in Figure 1; set aside.

2. Cut a 27" x 32" rectangle white print. Fold and press to mark center of each edge.

3. Prepare pattern pieces for bear and ribbon. Trace on the paper side of the fusible transfer web; cut out leaving a margin around each piece. **Note:** *Trace ribbon pieces first. Use areas around ribbon pieces to trace remaining pieces.*

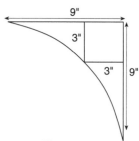

Figure 1
Trim round corner
shape as shown.

4. Fuse to the back of fabrics as directed on pattern pieces. Cut out each piece on traced line; remove paper backing.

5. Transfer detail lines to appliqué pieces using chalk pencil.

6. Arrange bear pieces in numerical order on white print rectangle as shown in Figure 2; fuse in place. Set aside ribbon pieces.

7. Place fabric stabilizer behind bear shape. Using machine-embroidery thread in the top of the machine and all-purpose thread in the bobbin, machine satin-stitch around fused pieces. Machine satin-stitch detail lines on bear using black machine-embroidery thread and on hair

bow using pink machine-embroidery thread. Remove fabric stabilizer.

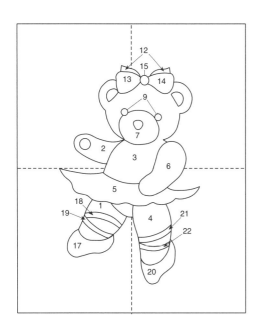

Figure 2
Arrange bear pieces on white print rectangle.

8. Prepare muslin side and end arch pieces as directed on pattern pieces. Transfer stitching lines to each piece.

9. From each dot fabric, cut two strips 3" by fabric width.

10. Foundation-piece arch pieces, randomly stitching dot fabrics to cover each muslin arch piece as shown in Figure 3. Trim edges even with muslin pieces.

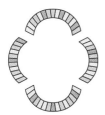   

Figure 3
Randomly cover muslin arch pieces with dot fabrics.

Figure 4
Join arch pieces to complete arch border.

11. Join arch pieces on short ends to complete arch border as shown in Figure 4.

12. Remove seam allowance from ends of arch pattern pieces. Cut fusible transfer web pieces as directed on pattern pieces; fuse to the back of each corresponding section of the arch border.

13. Place arch border on appliquéd rectangle,

centering bear design in border opening. Trace arch border outside edge on rectangle using chalk pencil; trim rectangle 1" inside traced line as shown in Figure 5.

Figure 5
Trim rectangle 1"
inside traced arch
border line.

14. Center trimmed rectangle on pink floral background piece; pin in place. Remove paper backing from arch border; place arch border on trimmed rectangle and fuse in place.

15. Place fabric stabilizer behind arch border. Using pastel-variegated rayon thread in the top of the machine and all-purpose thread in the bobbin; machine satin-stitch around inside and outside edge of arch border. Remove fabric stabilizer.

16. Cut away pink floral background behind white print center section close to inside arch stitching line.

17. Arrange ribbon pieces on background piece as shown in Figure 6; fuse in place.

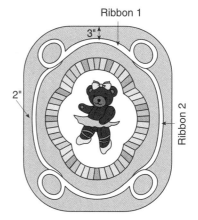

Figure 6
Arrange ribbon pieces on
background as shown.

18. Place fabric stabilizer behind ribbon pieces. Machine satin-stitch in place using white machine-embroidery thread in the top of the machine and all-purpose thread in the bobbin. Remove fabric stabilizer.

19. Place white eyelet ruffle right sides together

along edge of background piece; machine-baste 1/8" from edge.

20. Place prepared backing piece wrong side against quilter's fleece piece. Place appliquéd top right sides together with backing piece; pin in place. Trim backing and batting even with appliquéd top.

21. Stitch all around outside edge, leaving a 6" opening on one side. Turn right side out through opening; hand-stitch opening closed. Lightly press edge flat.

22. Hand- or machine-quilt as desired to finish. **Note:** *The sample shown was machine-quilted in a meandering pattern in white print center section using white machine-quilting thread in the top of the machine and all-purpose thread in the bobbin and in the pink floral background section using pink machine-quilting thread.* ❖

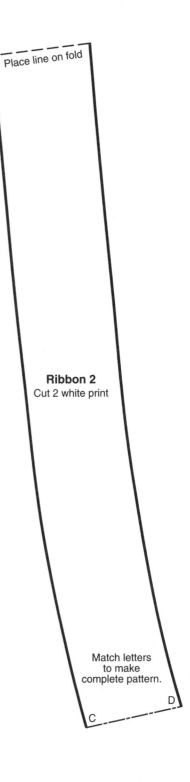

Place line on fold

Ribbon 2
Cut 2 white print

Match letters
to make
complete pattern.

C   D

Little Ballerina
Placement Diagram
35" x 50"

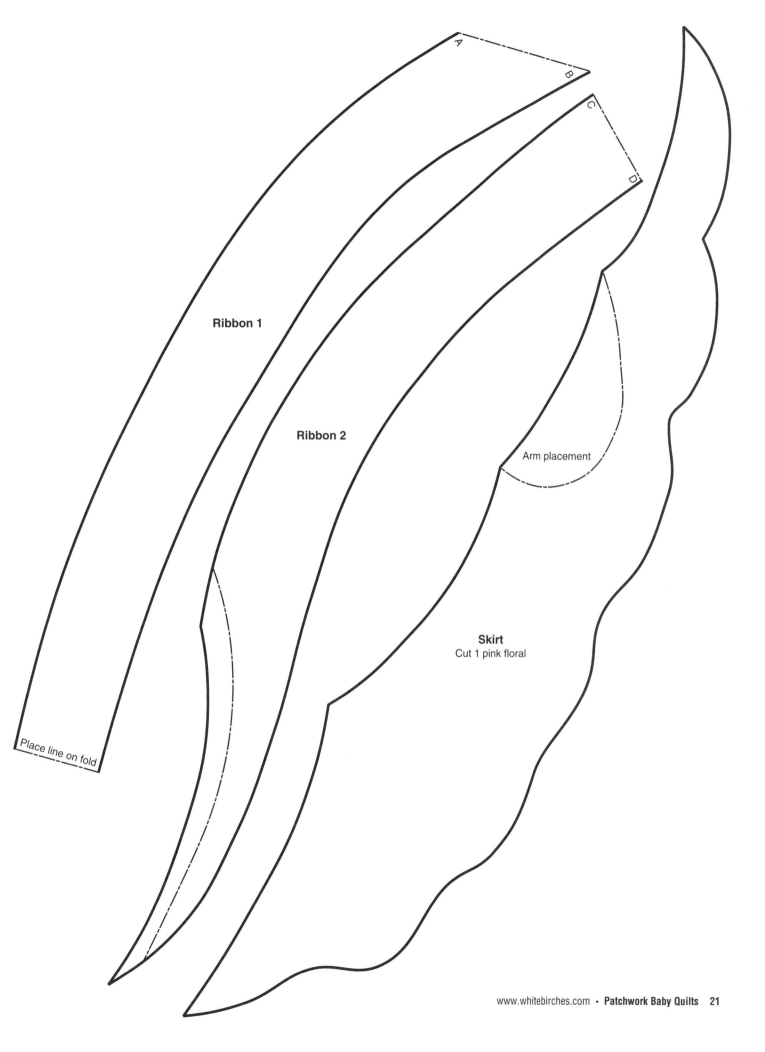

Ribbon 1

Ribbon 2

A

B

C

D

Arm placement

Skirt
Cut 1 pink floral

Place line on fold

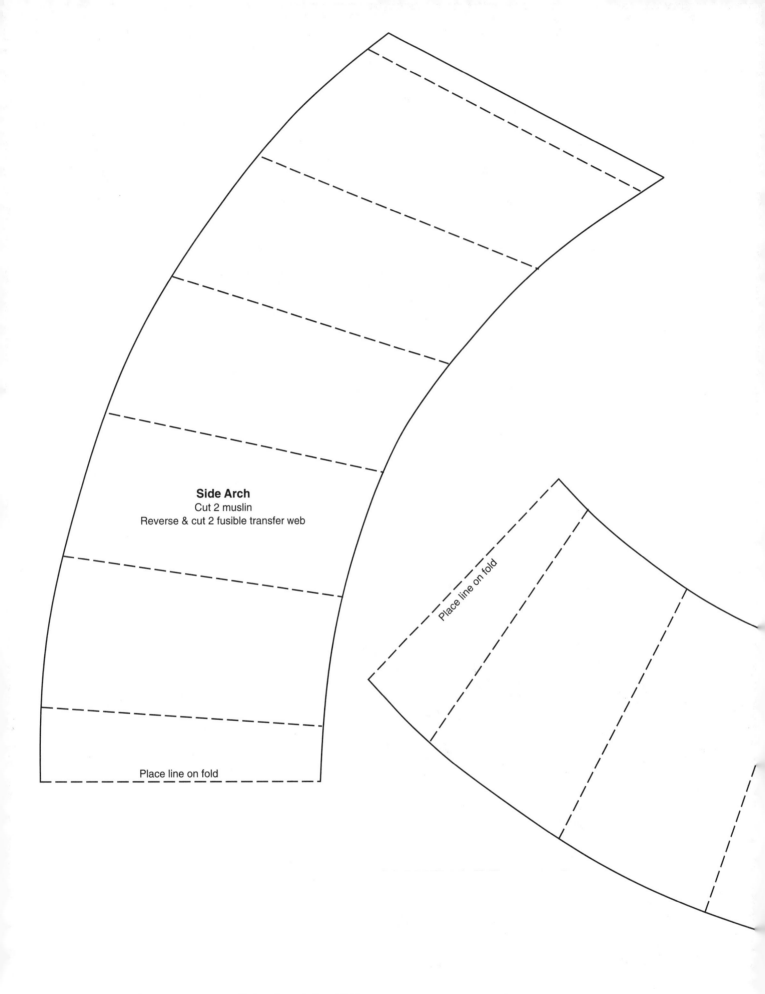

Side Arch
Cut 2 muslin
Reverse & cut 2 fusible transfer web

Place line on fold

Place line on fold

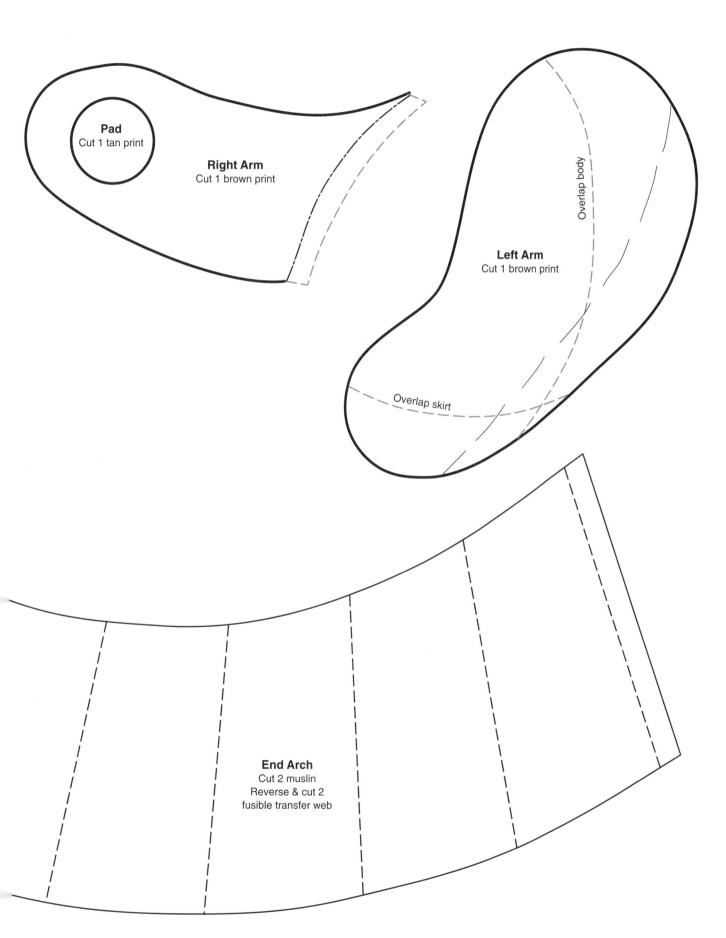

Pad
Cut 1 tan print

Right Arm
Cut 1 brown print

Left Arm
Cut 1 brown print

Overlap body

Overlap skirt

End Arch
Cut 2 muslin
Reverse & cut 2
fusible transfer web

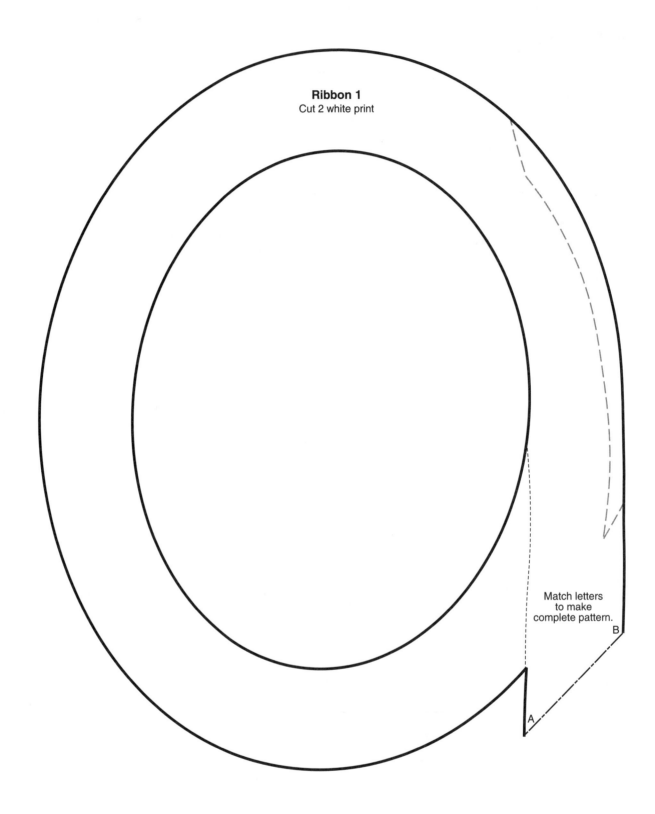

Ribbon 1
Cut 2 white print

Match letters
to make
complete pattern.

A

B

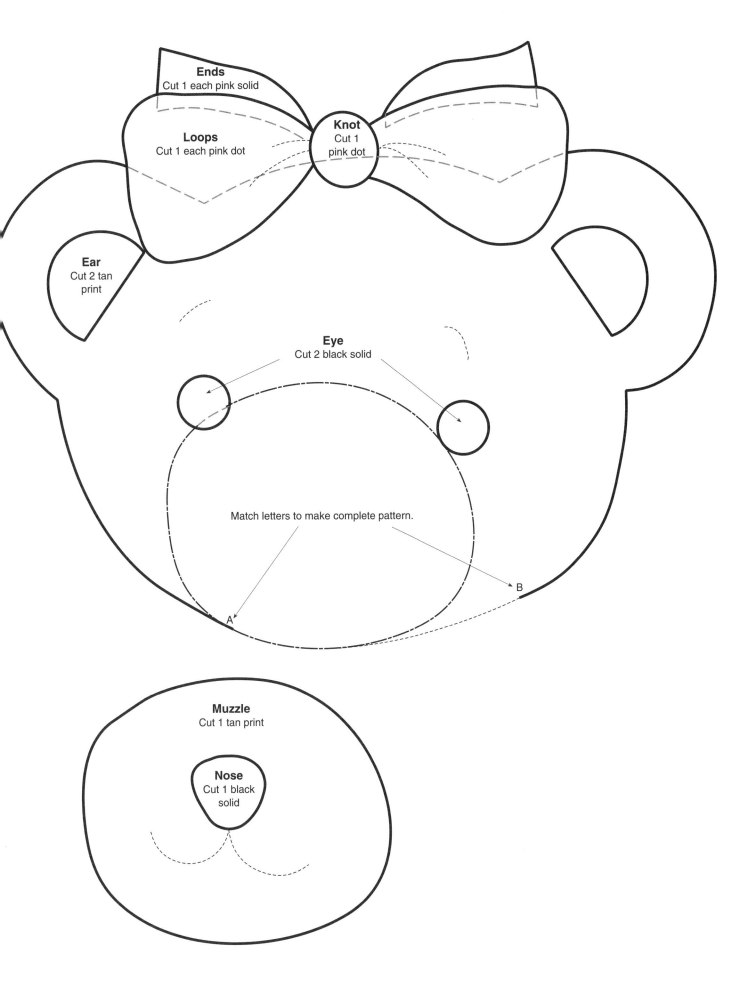

Ends
Cut 1 each pink solid

Loops
Cut 1 each pink dot

Knot
Cut 1
pink dot

Ear
Cut 2 tan
print

Eye
Cut 2 black solid

Match letters to make complete pattern.

A

B

Muzzle
Cut 1 tan print

Nose
Cut 1 black
solid

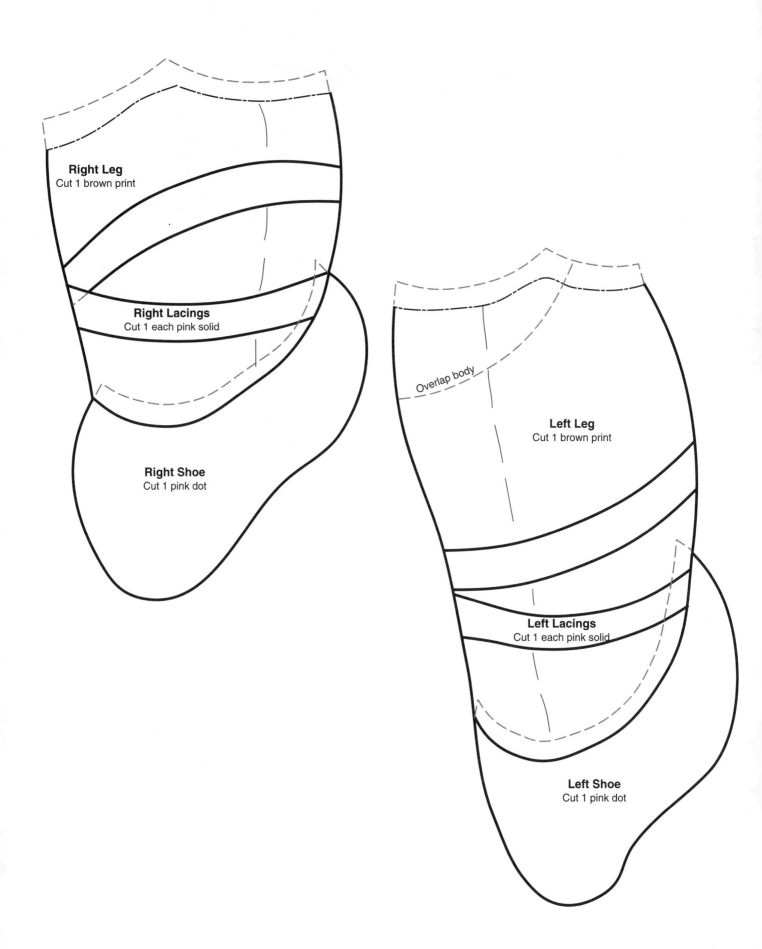

Right Leg
Cut 1 brown print

Right Lacings
Cut 1 each pink solid

Right Shoe
Cut 1 pink dot

Overlap body

Left Leg
Cut 1 brown print

Left Lacings
Cut 1 each pink solid

Left Shoe
Cut 1 pink dot

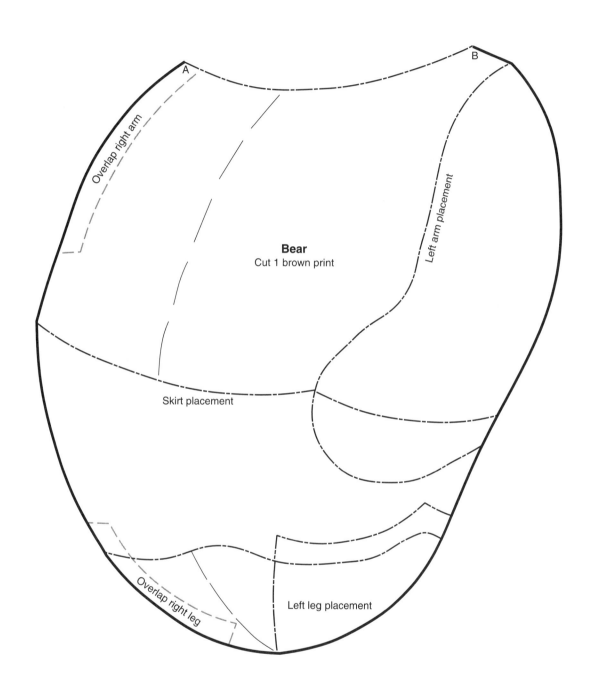

A

B

Overlap right arm

Left arm placement

Bear
Cut 1 brown print

Skirt placement

Overlap right leg

Left leg placement

Strippy Whirligigs

Purchase light, medium and dark fabrics or use up those leftover bits and pieces of aqua and peach prints to make this scrappy-looking quilt.

Project Notes

To avoid bias edges on the outside of the blocks in this quilt, bias strips are joined for the B triangle pieces. There will be large sections left from the rectangles cut for the bias strips. Plan other projects to match the quilt as a way to use these sections.

Project Specifications

Quilt Size: 34" x 50"
Block Size: 8" x 8"
Number of Blocks: 15

Fabrics & Batting

- 1 yard each light, medium and dark aqua and peach
- 3/4 yard white-on-white print
- 1/2 yard white-on-aqua dot
- Backing 38" x 54"
- Quilter's fleece 38" x 54"

Tools & Supplies

- All-purpose thread to match fabrics
- Basic sewing tools and supplies, rotary cutter, mat and ruler

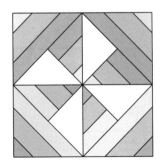

Whirligig
8" x 8" Block

Instructions

1. Make templates for A and B pattern pieces given, transferring lines on patterns to templates.

2. Cut an 18" x 30" rectangle each from the aqua and peach prints.

3. Cut seven 1 1/2"-wide bias strips from each light and dark print rectangle as shown in Figure 1. Cut seven 1 5/8"-wide bias strips from each medium print rectangle.

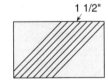

Figure 1
Cut bias strips as shown.

Figure 2
Join aqua print strips
to make a strip set.

4. Join one strip each light, medium and dark aqua print to make a strip set as shown in Figure 2; repeat for seven strip sets.

5. Place the B template on a strip set, aligning lines on template with seam lines of strip set as shown in Figure 3. Mark B1 piece on strip set; turn template and place next to marked piece as shown in Figure 4. Mark B2 piece; continue to mark B1

and B2 pieces down length of strip set; repeat on remaining strip sets to cut 15 each B1 and B2 aqua pieces.

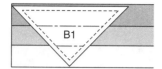

Figure 3
Place B template on strip set to mark B1 piece.

6. Repeat steps 4 and 5 with peach print strips to cut 15 each B1 and B2 peach pieces.

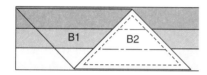

Figure 4
Place B template on strip set to mark B2 piece.

7. Cut two strips each light and dark aqua and peach prints 1 1/2" by fabric width. Cut two strips each medium aqua and peach prints 1 5/8" by fabric width.

8. Join one strip each light, medium and dark aqua print to make a strip set as shown in Figure 2; repeat for two strip sets.

9. Place the A template on a strip as for B pieces and referring to Figure 5. Cut 15 each A1 and A2 aqua pieces; repeat with peach print strips to cut 15 each A1 and A2 peach pieces.

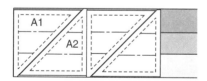

Figure 5
Place A template on strip set to mark A1 and A2 pieces.

10. Cut two strips 5 1/4" by fabric width white-on-white print; subcut each strip into 5 1/4" square segments. Cut each square on both diagonals to make C triangles. You will need 60 C triangles.

11. To piece one Whirligig block, sew an aqua A1 to C as shown in Figure 6; add an aqua B1 to make an aqua A1-B1 unit, again referring to Figure 6.

Figure 6
Sew A1 to C; add B1.

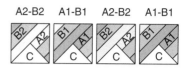

Figure 7
Make aqua and peach A-B units.

12. Repeat step 11 to make an aqua A2-B2 unit, a peach A1-B1 unit and a peach A2-B2 unit as shown in Figure 7.

13. Join the A-B units as shown in Figure 8 to complete one block; repeat to make 15 blocks.

Figure 8
Join the A-B units to complete 1 Whirligig block.

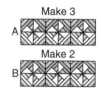

Figure 9
Join 3 blocks to make a row.

14. Join three blocks to make a block row A as shown in Figure 9; repeat for three rows.

15. Join three blocks to make a block row B, again referring to Figure 9; repeat for two rows.

16. Join the A and B block rows to complete the pieced center, beginning and ending with an A row as shown in Figure 10.

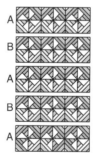

Figure 10
Join the A and B rows to complete the pieced center

Figure 11
Join aqua print strips to make a strip set.

17. Cut four strips each aqua and peach prints 1 1/2" by fabric width.

18. Join two strips each light, medium and dark aqua print to make a strip set as shown in Figure 11; repeat for two strip sets. Cut each strip set into 4 1/2" segments; you will need 12 aqua segments.

19. Repeat step 18 with peach print strips; you will need 10 peach segments.

20. Join four aqua segments and three peach segments to make a strip as shown in Figure 12; repeat. Join two each aqua and peach segments to make a strip, again referring to Figure 12; repeat.

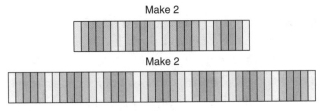

Figure 12
Join aqua and peach
segments to make a strip.

21. Cut two strips each white-on-white print 1 1/2" x 24 1/2" and 1 1/2" x 40 1/2".

22. Center and sew a longer pieced strip to a longer white-on-white print strip; trim pieced strip even

on both ends. Repeat with all pieced and white-on-white print strips.

23. Sew a longer strip to opposite long sides of the pieced center; press seams toward strips.

24. Cut four 5 1/2" x 5 1/2" squares white-on-white print. Sew a square to each end of the remaining strips. Sew a strip to the top and bottom of the pieced center to complete the top.

25. Sandwich quilter's fleece between the completed top and the prepared backing piece; pin or baste to hold.

26. Hand- or machine-quilt as desired. **Note:** *The sample shown was professionally machine-quilted in an allover meandering pattern.*

27. Remove pins or basting; trim edges even with top. Cut five strips 2 1/4" by fabric width white-on-aqua dot; join strips on short ends to make a long strip. Fold strip in half with wrong sides together; press to make binding strip. Bind edges of quilt to finish. ❖

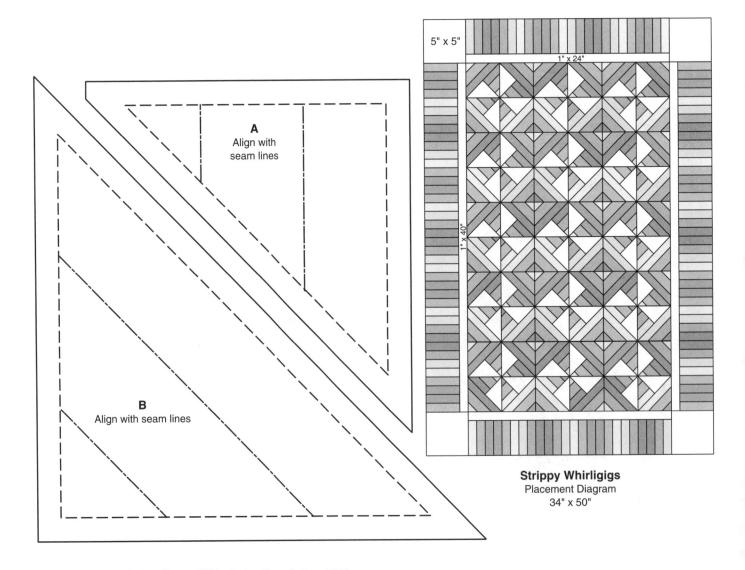

Strippy Whirligigs
Placement Diagram
34" x 50"

Four-Patch Pets

Kitties and puppies make cute first pets for Baby.

Project Specifications

Quilt Size: 35" x 50" (without ruffles)
Unit Size: 12" x 12"
Number of Units: 6

Fabrics & Batting

- 1/8 yard each pink and blue checks
- 1/4 yard each pink and blue solids
- 1/2 yard white print
- 1 yard pink/blue plaid
- 1 3/4 yards pink print
- Backing 39" x 54"
- Quilter's fleece 39" x 54"

Tools & Supplies

- All-purpose thread to match fabrics
- Pink-variegated and blue-variegated rayon thread
- Pink machine-quilting thread
- 1/2 yard fusible transfer web
- 3/4 yard fabric stabilizer
- Basic sewing tools and supplies, rotary cutter, mat and ruler

Instructions

1. Cut 12 squares 6 1/2" x 6 1/2" white print.
2. Prepare templates for pattern pieces given. Trace on paper side of fusible transfer web as directed on patterns for number needed. Cut out leaving a margin beyond traced line.
3. Fuse shapes on wrong side of fabrics as directed on patterns for color; cut out on marked line. Remove paper backing.
4. Arrange a cat shape on a white print square; fuse in place. Repeat with all cat and dog shapes.
5. Place a piece of fabric stabilizer behind fused shape. Machine satin-stitch around shape using

matching variegated rayon thread in the top of the machine and all-purpose thread in the bobbin. Machine satin-stitch detail lines. Remove fabric stabilizer.

6. Cut 12 squares 6 1/2" x 6 1/2" pink/blue plaid.
7. Sew a cat square to a pink/blue plaid square to make a row as shown in Figure 1; repeat for six rows, again referring to Figure 1.

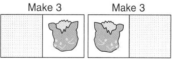

Figure 1
Sew a cat square to a plaid
square to make a row.

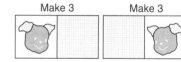

Figure 2
Sew a dog square to a
plaid square to make a row.

8. Sew a dog square to a pink/blue plaid square to make a row as shown in Figure 2; repeat for six rows, again referring to Figure 2.
9. Sew a cat row to a dog row to make a Four-Patch unit referring to the Placement Diagram for positioning of rows; repeat to make six Four-Patch units.
10. Cut seven 3 1/2" x 12 1/2" strips pink print for sashing strips; cut two 3 1/2" x 3 1/2" squares white print for sashing squares.

11. Join two Four-Patch units with one sashing strip to make a unit row as shown in Figure 3; repeat for three unit rows.

3 1/2" x 12 1/2"

Make 2

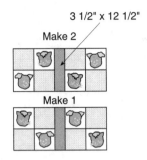

Make 1

Figure 3
Join 2 Four-Patch units with 1
sashing strip to make a unit row.

12. Join two sashing strips with one sashing square to make a sashing row as shown in Figure 4; repeat for two sashing rows.

3 1/2" x 12 1/2"   3 1/2" x 3 1/2"

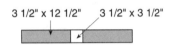

Figure 4
Join 2 sashing strips with 1 sashing
square to make a sashing row.

13. Join unit rows with sashing rows beginning and ending with a unit row and referring to the Placement Diagram for positioning of rows.

14. Cut two strips each 4 1/2" x 27 1/2" and 4 1/2" x 42 1/2" pink print. Sew a longer strip to opposite long sides of the pieced center; press seams toward strips.

15. Cut eight 2 1/2" x 2 1/2" squares each white print and pink/blue plaid. Join one square each fabric to make a row; repeat for eight rows. Join two rows to make a Four-Patch unit as shown in Figure 5; repeat for four Four-Patch units.

Figure 5
Join squares to make
a Four-Patch unit.

16. Sew a Four-Patch unit to each end of the remaining pink print strips; sew a strip to the top and bottom of the pieced center to complete the top.

17. Cut eight strips pink/blue plaid 2 1/8" x 40". Place two strips wrong sides together; stitch

across short edges using 1/8" seam allowance. Fold strips back and align with right sides together; stitch across same edge using a 1/4" seam allowance as shown in Figure 6, enclosing previous seam. Repeat on all short edges to make a joined tube; press seams in one direction.

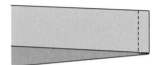

Figure 6
Stitch across short edges using 1/4" seam
allowance to enclose previous seam.

18. Turn under one edge of tube 1/8"; turn under again 1/4" and press. Topstitch along folded edge to hem.

19. Cut eight strips pink print 3 5/8" x 40". Join strips and hem edge as for pink/blue plaid strip.

20. Place pink/blue plaid strip with wrong side against right side of pink print strip with raw edges aligned as shown in Figure 7. Sew a double row of basting stitches along raw edge through both strips.

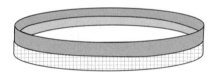

Figure 7
Place tubes together, aligning raw edges.

21. Gather strips to make ruffle to fit around edge of completed top; pin ruffle right sides together with completed top with raw edges aligned. Baste in place using a 1/8" seam allowance.

22. Place prepared backing piece on quilter's fleece; place top right sides together with backing piece with ruffle on inside. Pin in place.

23. Stitch all around edge, leaving a 10" opening on one side. Turn right side out through opening; hand-stitch opening closed.

24. Hand- or machine-quilt as desired to finish. Note: *The sample shown was machine-quilted in an allover meandering pattern using pink machine-quilting thread in the top of the machine and all-purpose thread in the bobbin.* ❖

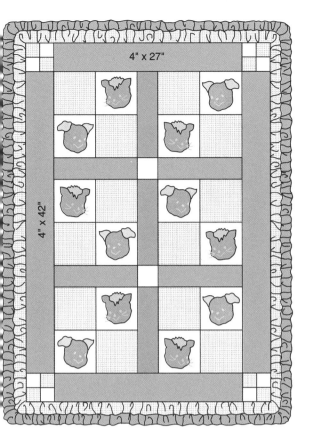

Four-Patch Pets
Placement Diagram
35" x 50"
(without ruffles)

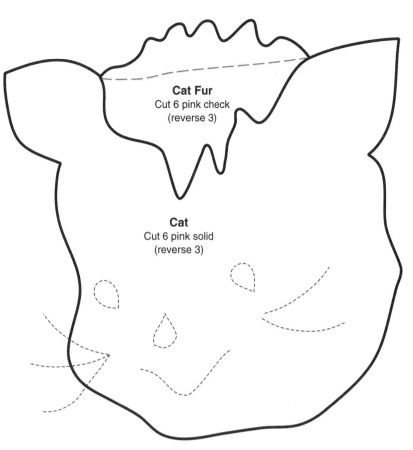

Cat Fur
Cut 6 pink check
(reverse 3)

Cat
Cut 6 pink solid
(reverse 3)

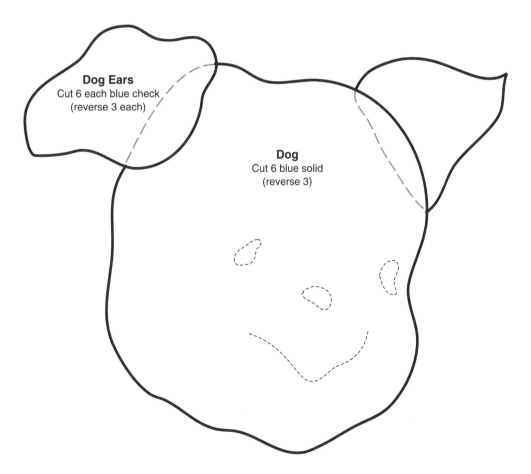

Dog Ears
Cut 6 each blue check
(reverse 3 each)

Dog
Cut 6 blue solid
(reverse 3)

Sleepyhead Bear

This tired little bear needs his own quilt at bedtime. Who knows? It may become Baby's favorite sleepy-time cuddler, too.

Project Specifications

Quilt Size: 38" x 55"
Block Size: 6" x 6"
Number of Blocks: 16

Fabrics & Batting

- Scrap each red and black prints
- Fat quarter each 8 prints
- 1/4 yard blue plaid
- 3/8 yard brown print
- 1 1/2 yards cream print
- 1/2 yard cream flannel
- Backing 42" x 59"
- Quilter's fleece 42" x 59"

Tools & Supplies

- All-purpose thread to match fabrics
- Black, medium brown and cream machine-quilting thread
- 3/4 yard fusible transfer web
- 5/8 yard fabric stabilizer
- Basting spray
- Basic sewing tools and supplies, chalk pencil, rotary cutter, mat and ruler

Instructions

1. Cut a 17 1/2" x 30 1/2" rectangle cream print.

2. Prepare pattern pieces for bear body, legs, right arm and hat. Trace on the paper side of the fusible transfer web; cut out leaving a margin around each piece.

3. Fuse to the back of fabrics as directed on pattern pieces. Cut out each piece on traced line; remove paper backing. Transfer detail lines to appliqué pieces using chalk pencil.

4. Prepare template for left arm; cut as directed on piece. Cut away seam allowance and center section from template as directed on pattern to make two templates as shown in Figure 1. Reverse resulting templates and trace one upper arm piece and one lower arm piece on the paper side of the fusible transfer web. Cut out on traced line.

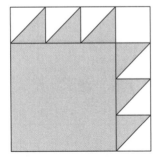

Bear Paw
6" x 6" Block

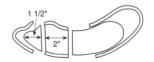

Figure 1
Cut away seam allowance and
center section to make 2 templates.

5. Place brown print pieces right sides together; stitch all around outside edge. Cut small slit in upper center of backside; turn right side out through slit. Press edges flat.

6. Place fusible transfer web pieces on backside of arm piece; fuse in place. Remove paper backing.

7. Arrange bear and hat pieces on cream print rectangle as shown in Figure 2; fuse in place.

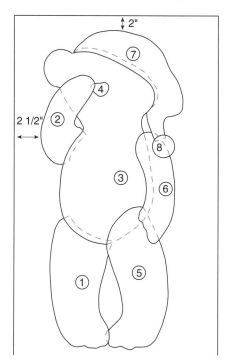

Figure 2
Arrange bear and hat pieces in numerical order as shown.

Figure 3
Leave unfused arm section free to form opening.

8. Place fabric stabilizer behind bear shape. Using black machine-quilting thread in the top of the machine and all-purpose thread in the bobbin, machine buttonhole-stitch around fused pieces. *Note: Do not stitch unfused section of arm; leave free to form opening as shown in Figure 3.* Machine satin-stitch detail lines. Remove fabric stabilizer.

9. From each print fat quarter, cut two strips 2 1/2" x 22". Cut each strip randomly into 4"- to 9"-long pieces.

10. Join random-length pieces on short ends to make a strip at least 230" long, alternating colors and strip lengths as shown in Figure 4; press seams in one direction.

Figure 4
Join random-length pieces on short ends to make a long strip.

11. Cut two strips from pieced strip 2 1/2" x 17 1/2". Sew a strip to the top and bottom of the appliquéd rectangle; press seams toward strips. Set aside remaining strip.

12. From each print fat quarter, cut two 5" x 5" squares for A and six 2 3/8" x 2 3/8" squares for B.

13. Cut three strips 2 3/8" by fabric width cream print; subcut into 2 3/8" squares for B.

14. Cut one strip 2" by fabric width cream print; subcut into 2" squares for C.

15. Draw a diagonal line on the wrong side of each cream print B square.

16. Place a cream B right sides together with a print B; stitch 1/4" on each side of the diagonal line as shown in Figure 5. Cut apart on the diagonal line and press seam allowance toward the print side to complete two B units. Repeat with all B squares.

Figure 5
Stitch 1/4" on each side of the diagonal line.

Figure 6
Join 3 B units.

17. To piece one Bear Paw block, join three B units as shown in Figure 6; repeat. Sew a B strip to a same-print A square as shown in Figure 7.

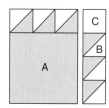

Figure 7
Join the B strips with A and C to complete 1 block.

18. Sew a C square to one end of the remaining B strip; sew to the adjacent side of the A square, again referring to Figure 7 to complete one block. Repeat to make 16 blocks, two blocks of each print.

19. Cut one strip 5 1/8" by fabric width cream print; subcut into 5 1/8" square segments. Cut each square on one diagonal to make D triangles.

20. Cut two strips 9 3/4" by fabric width cream print; subcut into 9 3/4" square segments. Cut each square on both diagonals to make E triangles.

21. Join four blocks with four D and six E triangles to make a strip as shown in Figure 8; press seams toward triangles. Repeat to make four block strips.

Figure 8
Join 4 blocks with 4 D
and 6 E triangles.

22. Sew a block strip to opposite sides of the appliquéd rectangle referring to the Placement Diagram for positioning of strips. Sew the remaining block strips to the top and bottom to complete the pieced center.

23. Cut two strips each from the pieced strip 2 1/2" x 38 1/2" and 2 1/2" x 51 1/2". Sew the longer strips to opposite sides and the shorter strips to the top and bottom of the pieced center to complete the top.

24. Spray one side of the quilter's fleece with basting spray; place wrong side of prepared backing on the sprayed side. Repeat on opposite side of batting with completed top.

25. From each print fat quarter, cut one strip 2 1/2" x 22". Join three strips to make a strip set as shown in Figure 9; repeat. Join the remaining two strips to make a strip set. Press seams in one direction.

Figure 10
Join 1 segment from
each set to make a row.

Figure 9
Join strips to
make 3 strip sets.

26. Cut each strip set into eight 2 1/2" segments.

27. Join one segment from each set to make a row as shown in Figure 10. Repeat to make eight rows, alternating placement of each segment to result in a random arrangement of color. Join rows to make a pieced square.

28. Cut one 16 1/2" x 16 1/2" square cream flannel; place right sides together with pieced square. Stitch all around leaving a 6" opening on one side. Turn right side out through opening; hand-stitch opening closed. Press edges flat.

29. Hand- or machine-quilt sandwiched quilt and small pieced quilt as desired. Note: *The sample quilt shown was machine-quilted in the ditch of seams, 1/4" around bear and in a random pattern in cream print areas using cream machine-quilting thread in the top of the machine and all-purpose thread in the bobbin. The small pieced quilt was machine-quilted in the ditch of seams using medium brown machine-quilting thread in the top of the machine and all-purpose thread in the bobbin.*

30. Remove pins or basting. Cut five strips 2 1/4" by fabric width brown print; join strips on short ends to make a long strip. Fold strip in half with wrong sides together; press to make binding strip. Bind edges of quilt. Insert small quilt in opening in bear's left arm to finish. ❖

Sleepyhead Bear
Placement Diagram
38" x 55"

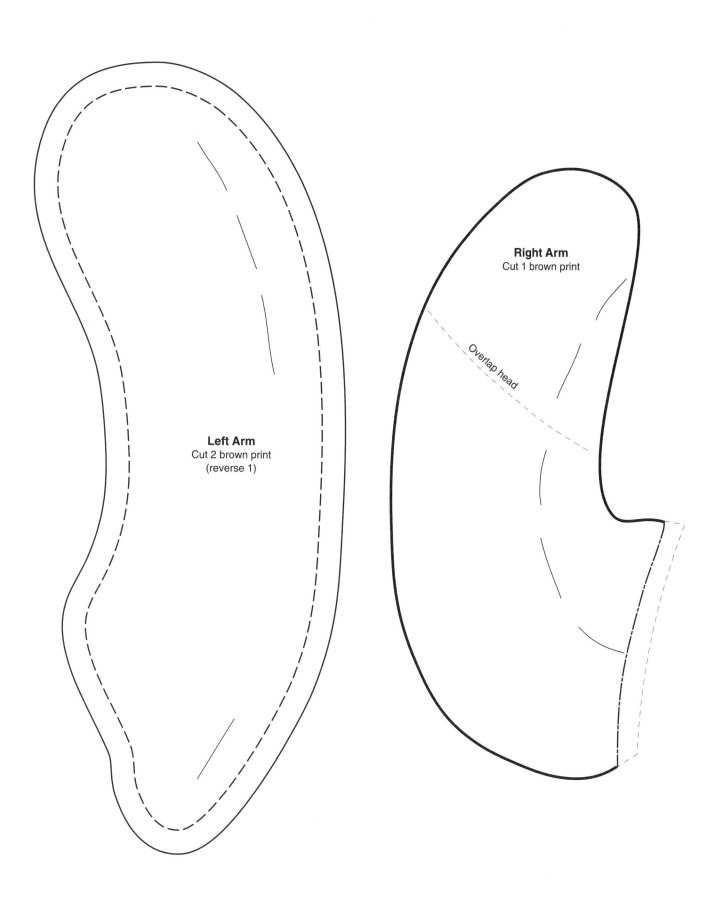

Left Arm
Cut 2 brown print
(reverse 1)

Right Arm
Cut 1 brown print

Overlap head

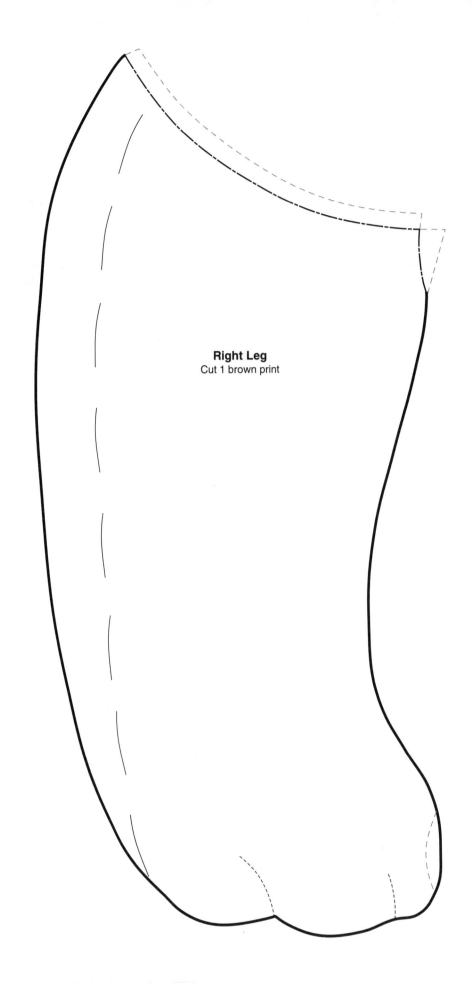

Right Leg
Cut 1 brown print

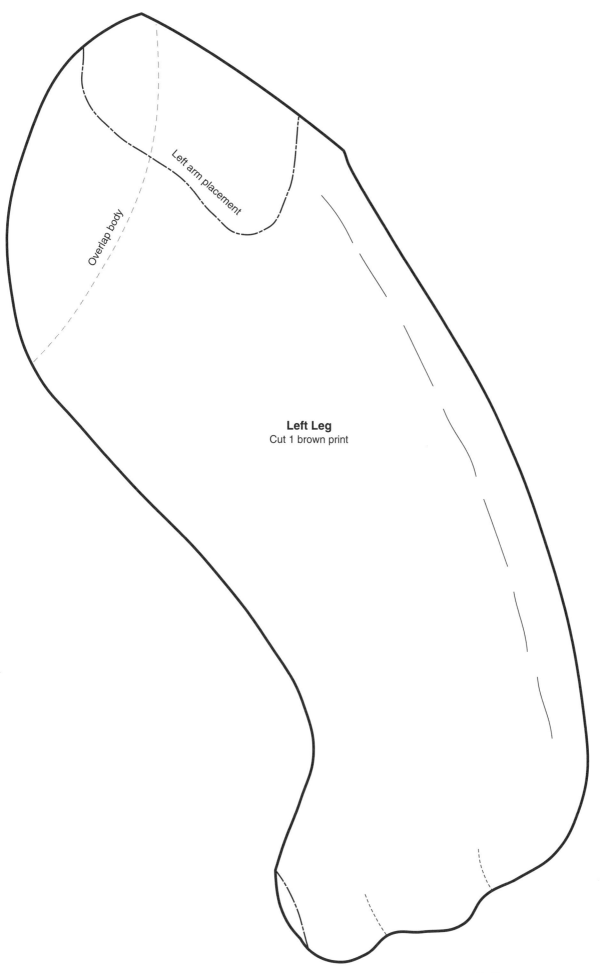

Overlap body

Left arm placement

Left Leg
Cut 1 brown print

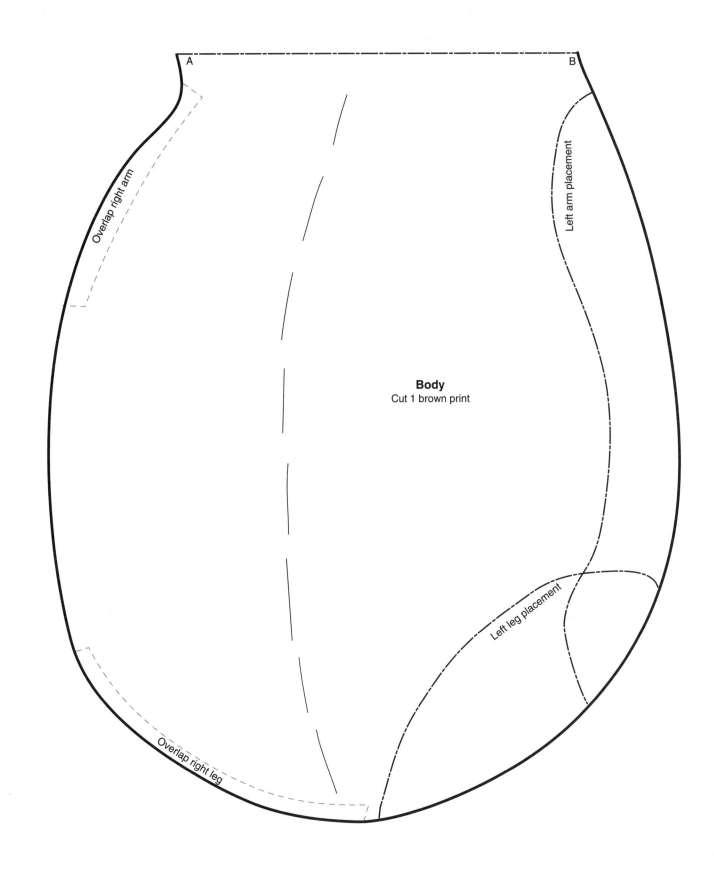

A

B

Overlap right arm

Left arm placement

Body
Cut 1 brown print

Left leg placement

Overlap right leg

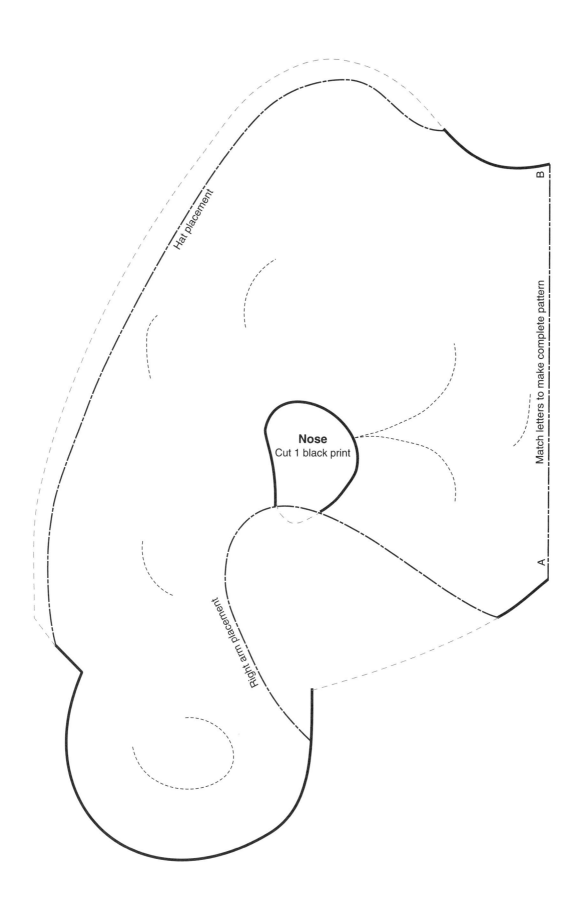

Hat placement

B

Match letters to make complete pattern

Nose
Cut 1 black print

A

Right arm placement

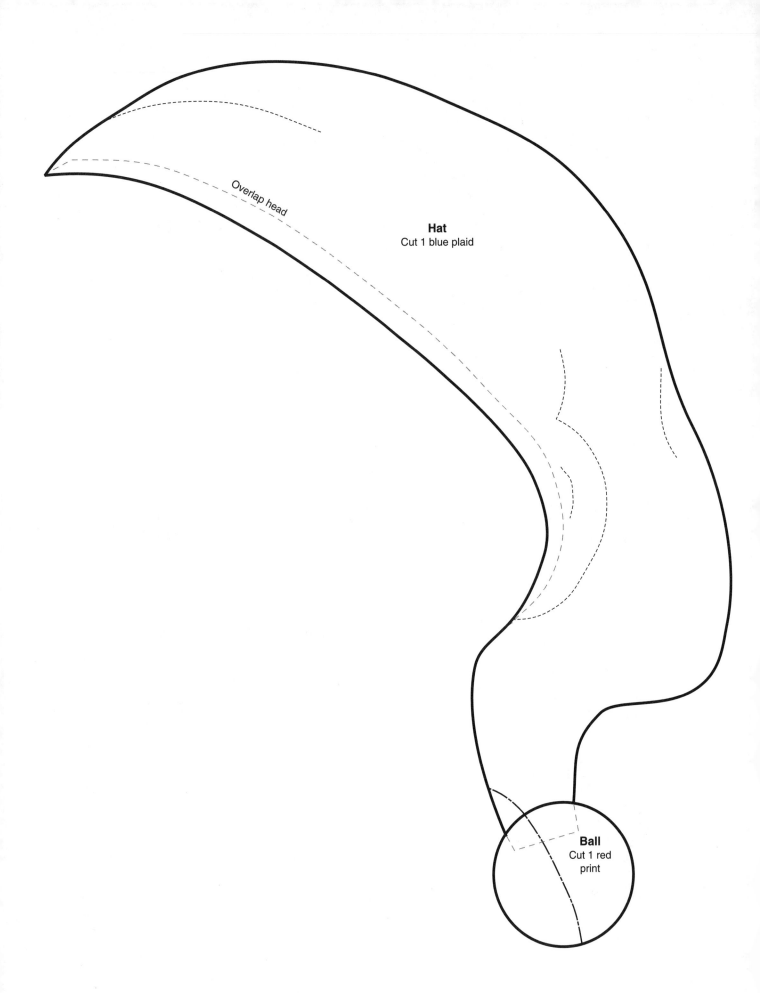

Hat
Cut 1 blue plaid

Overlap head

Ball
Cut 1 red
print